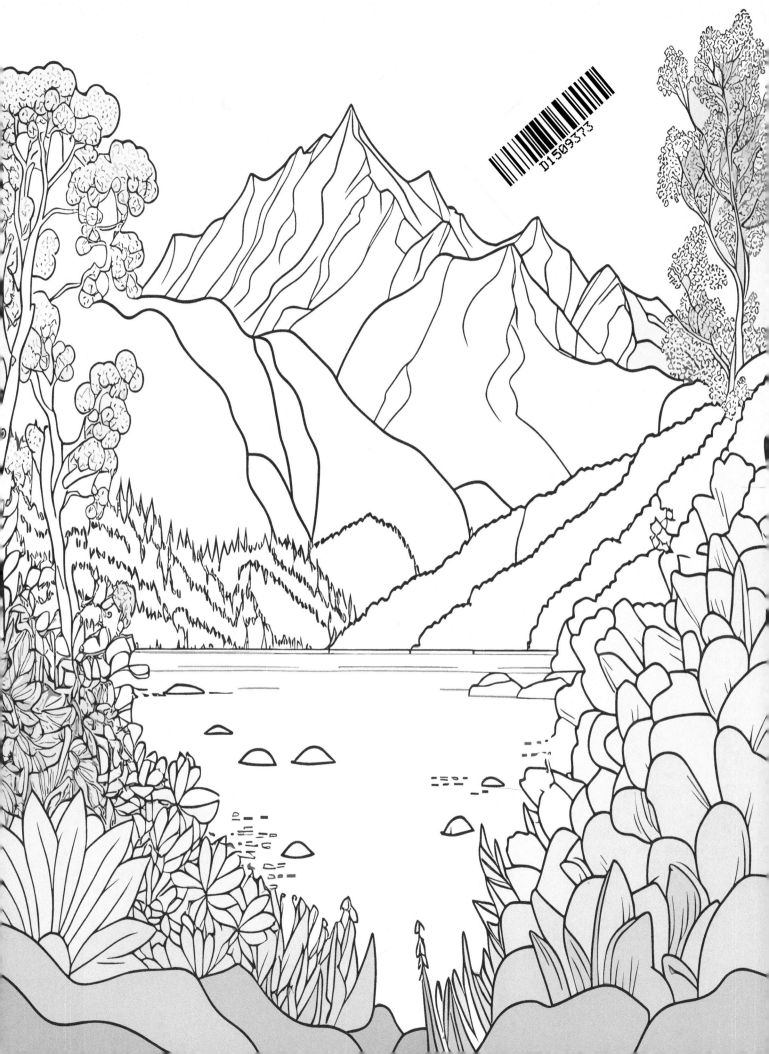

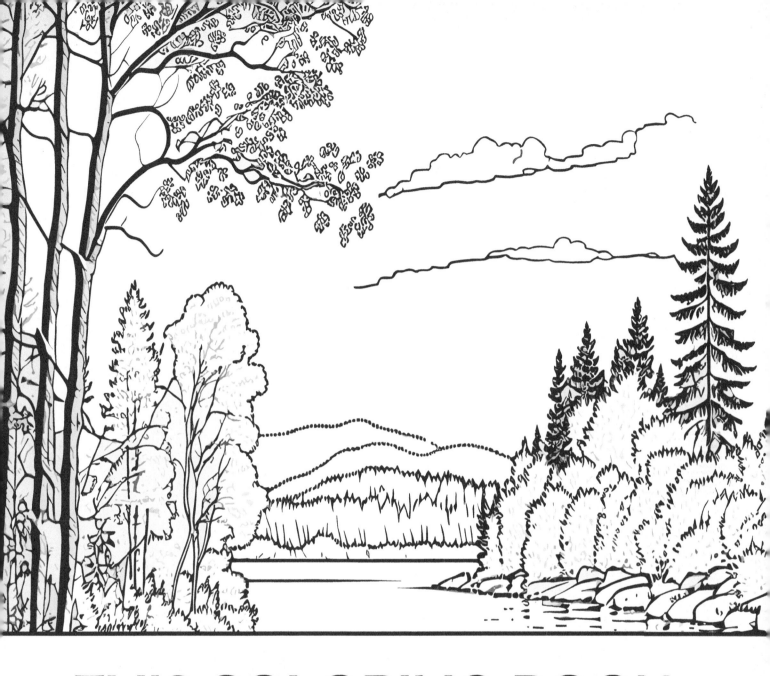

THIS COLORING BOOK BELONGS TO:

....

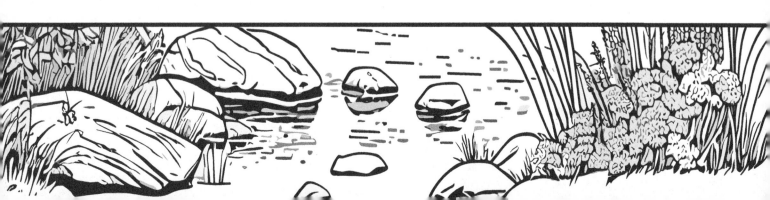

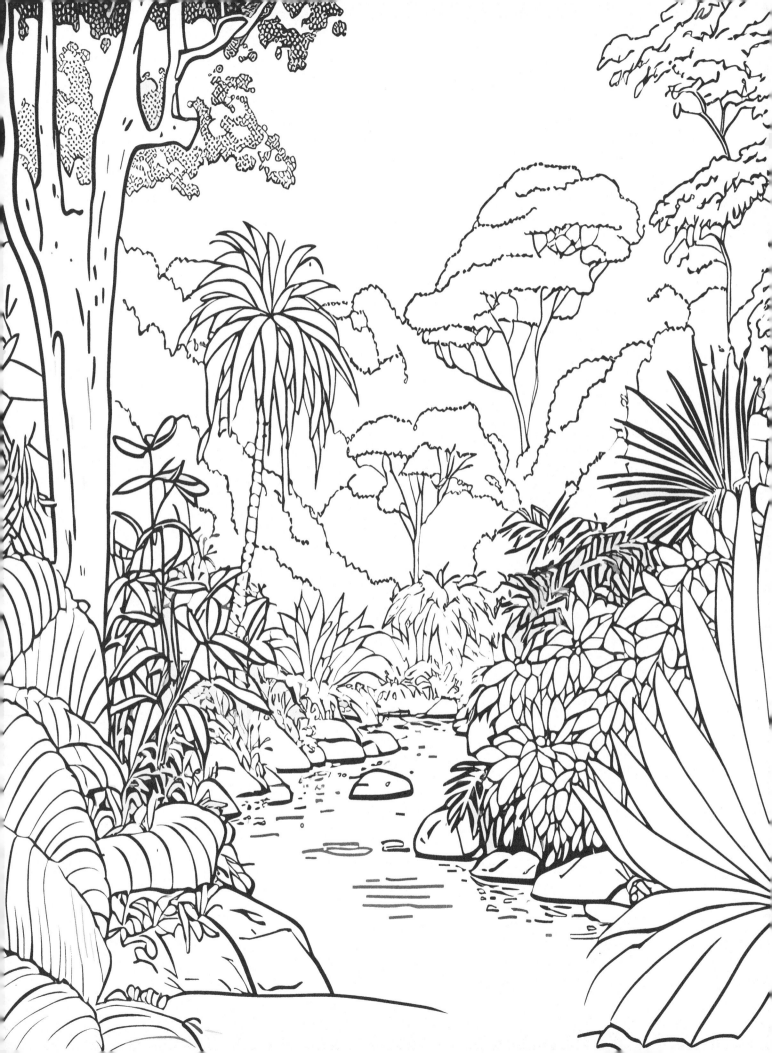

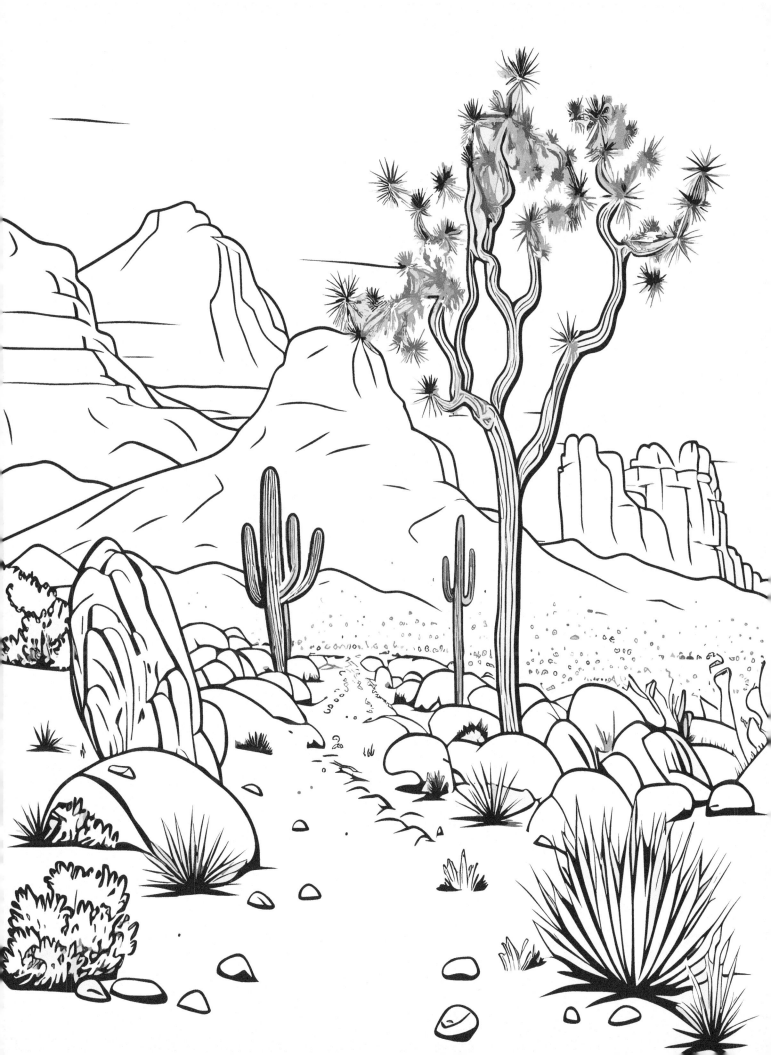

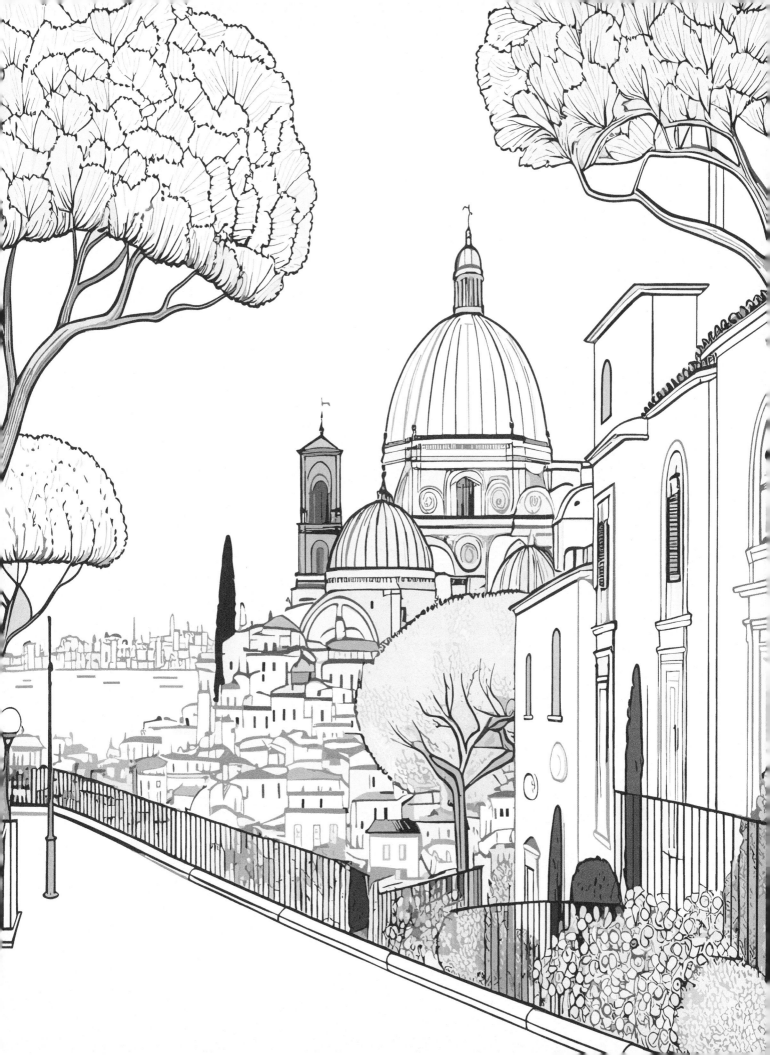

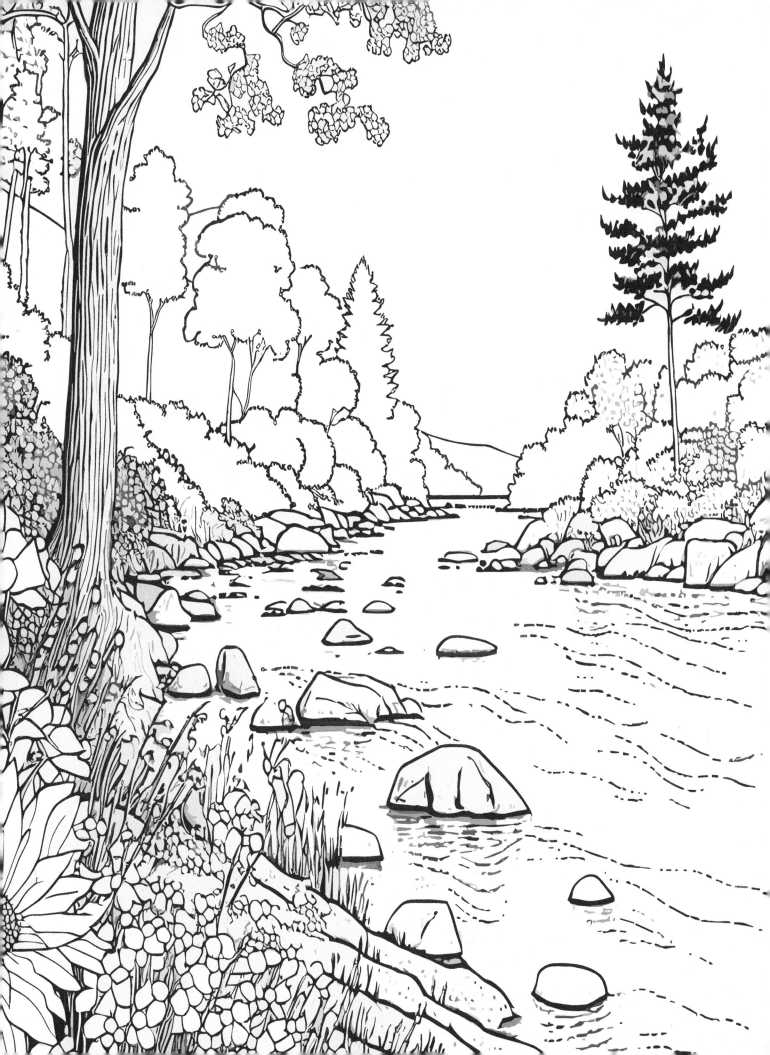

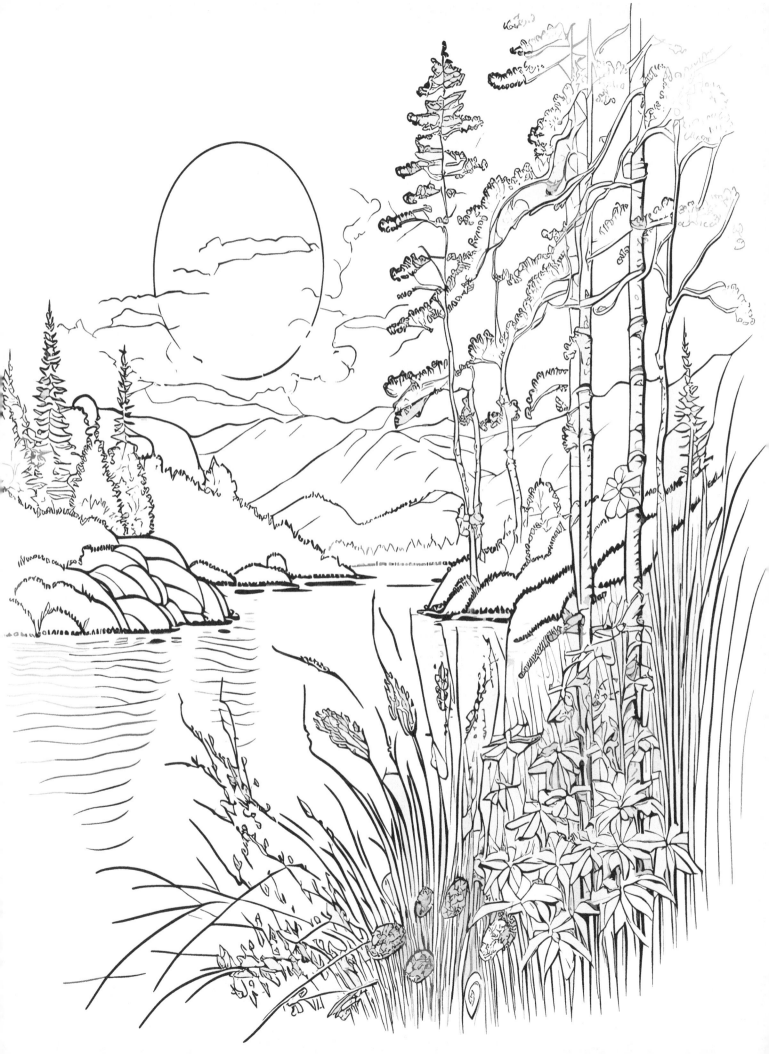

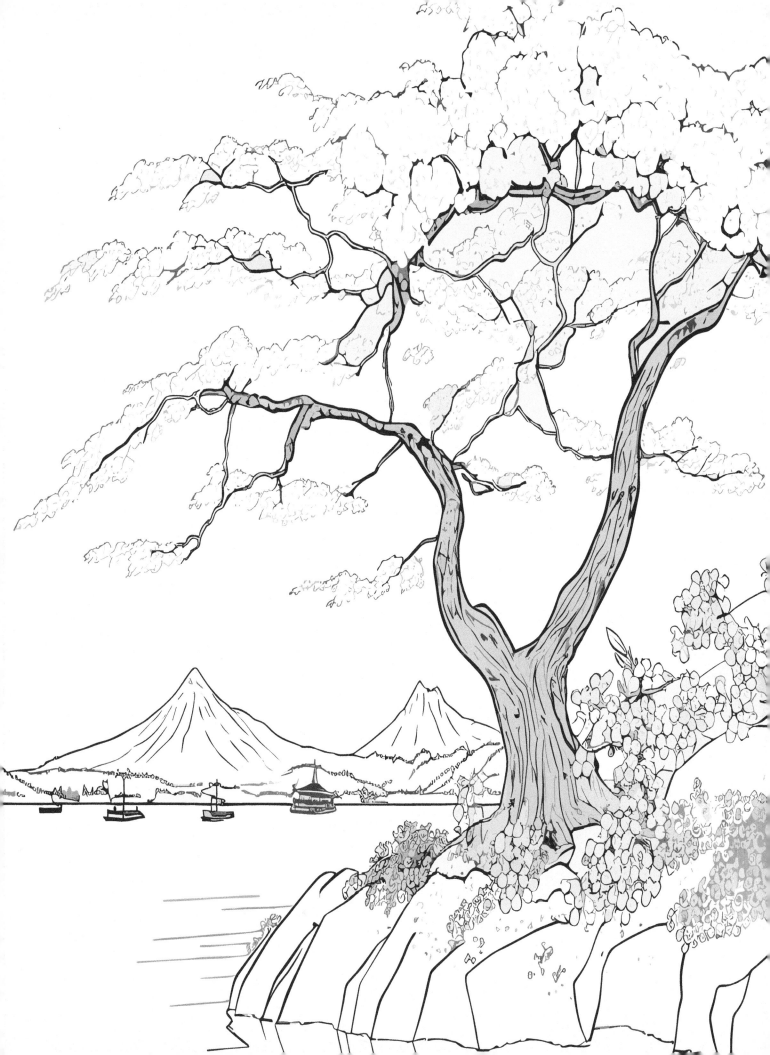

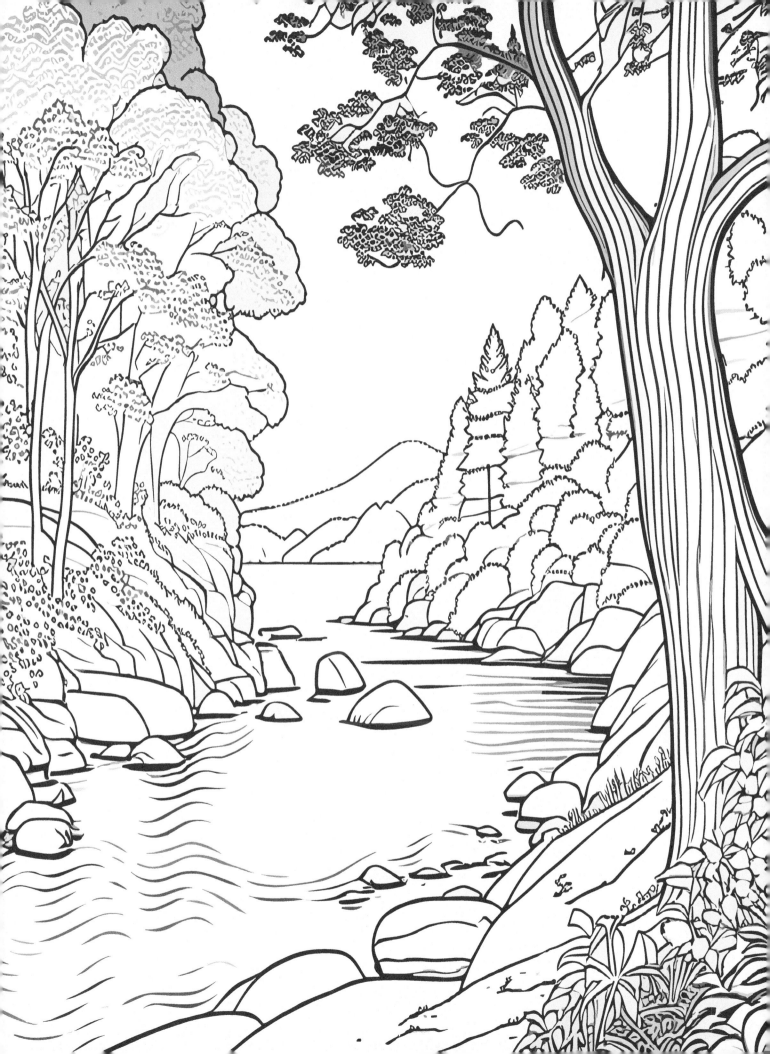

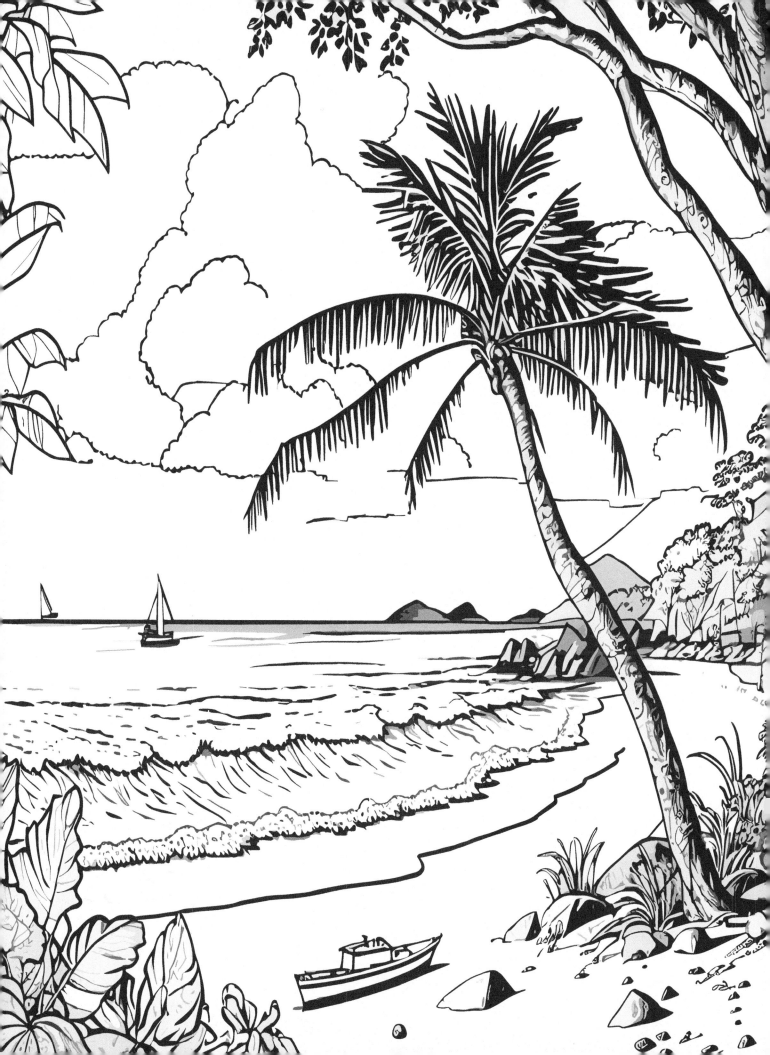

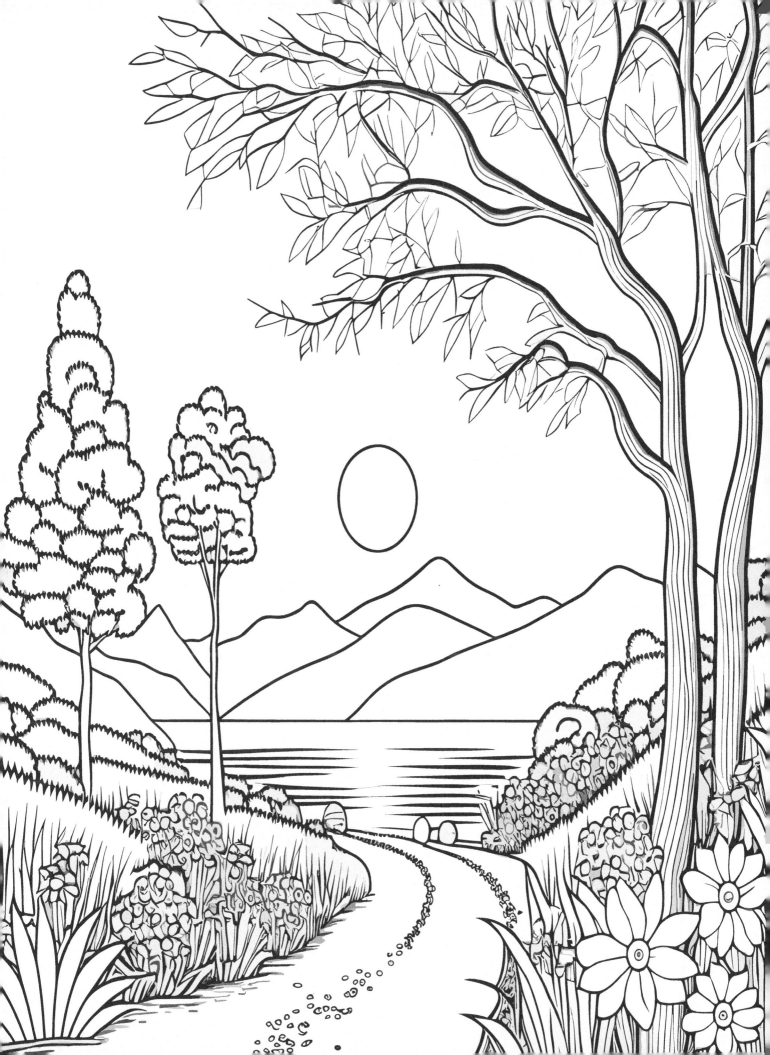

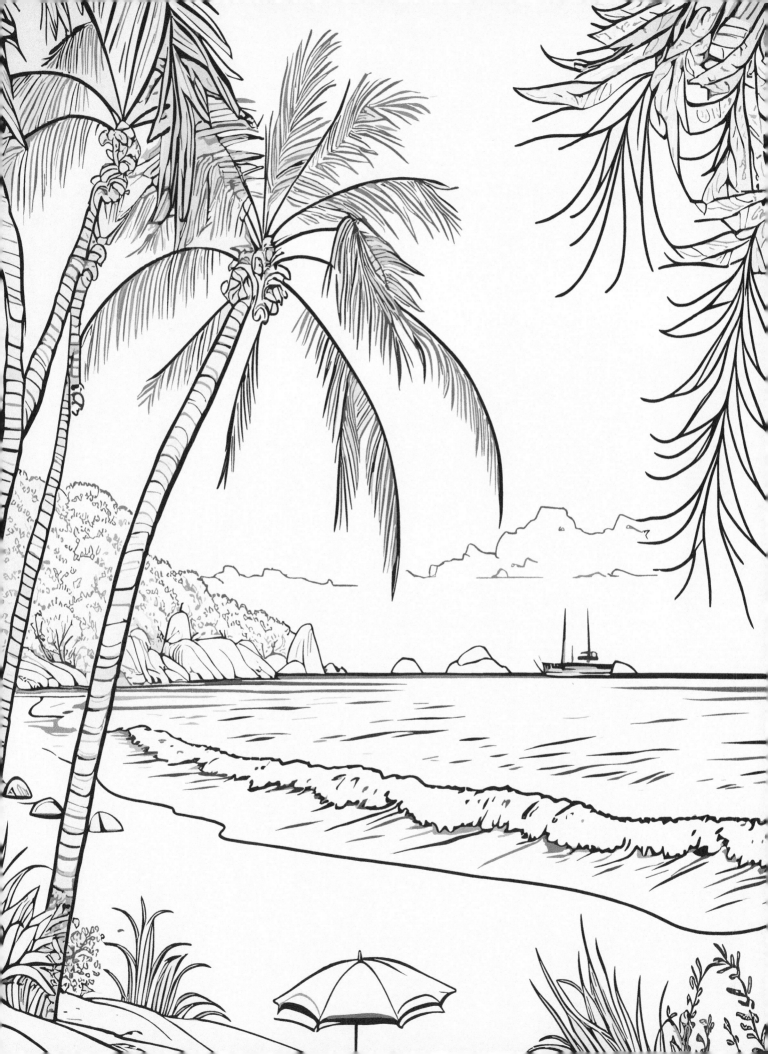

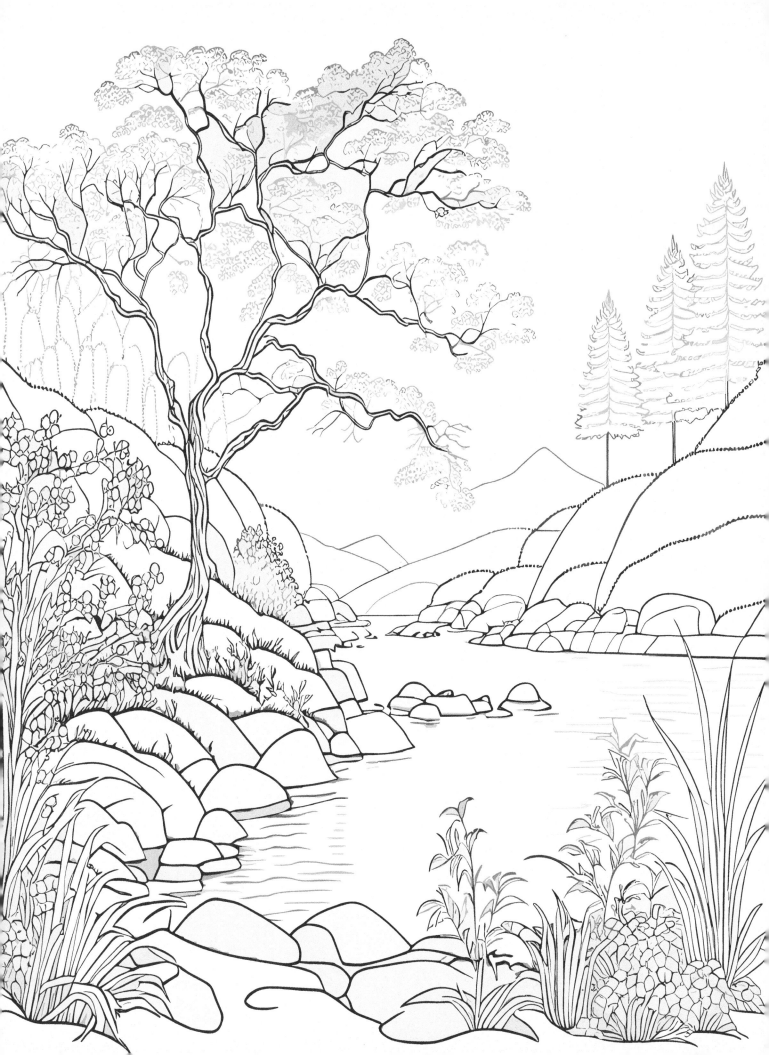

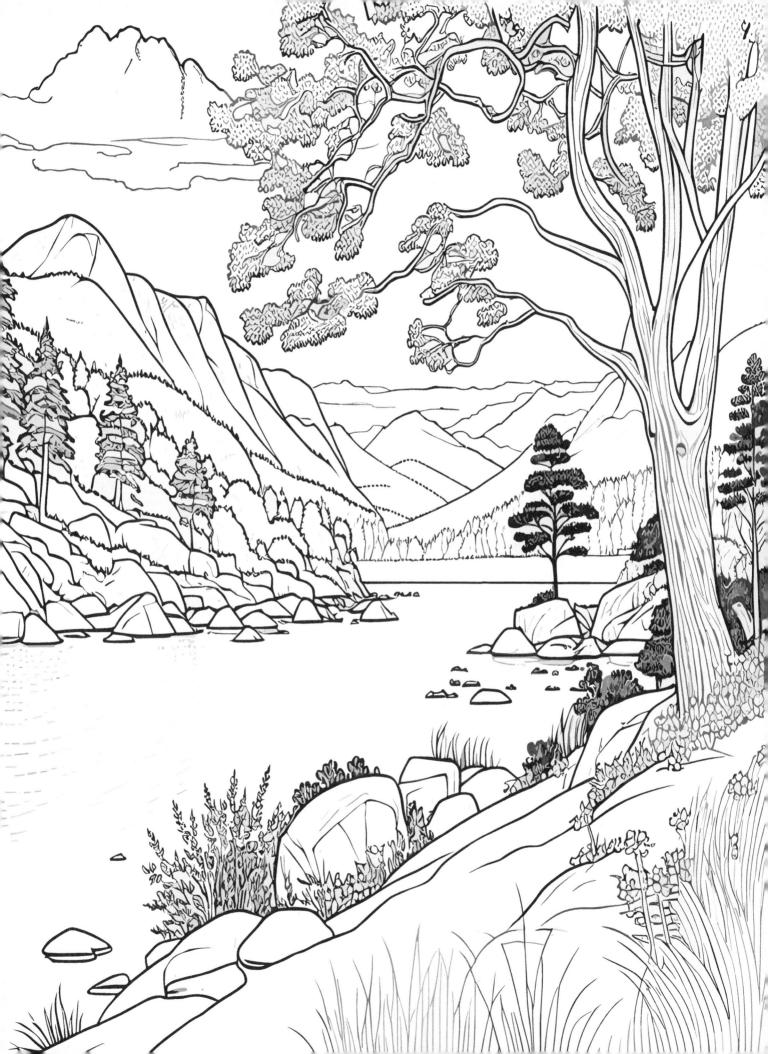

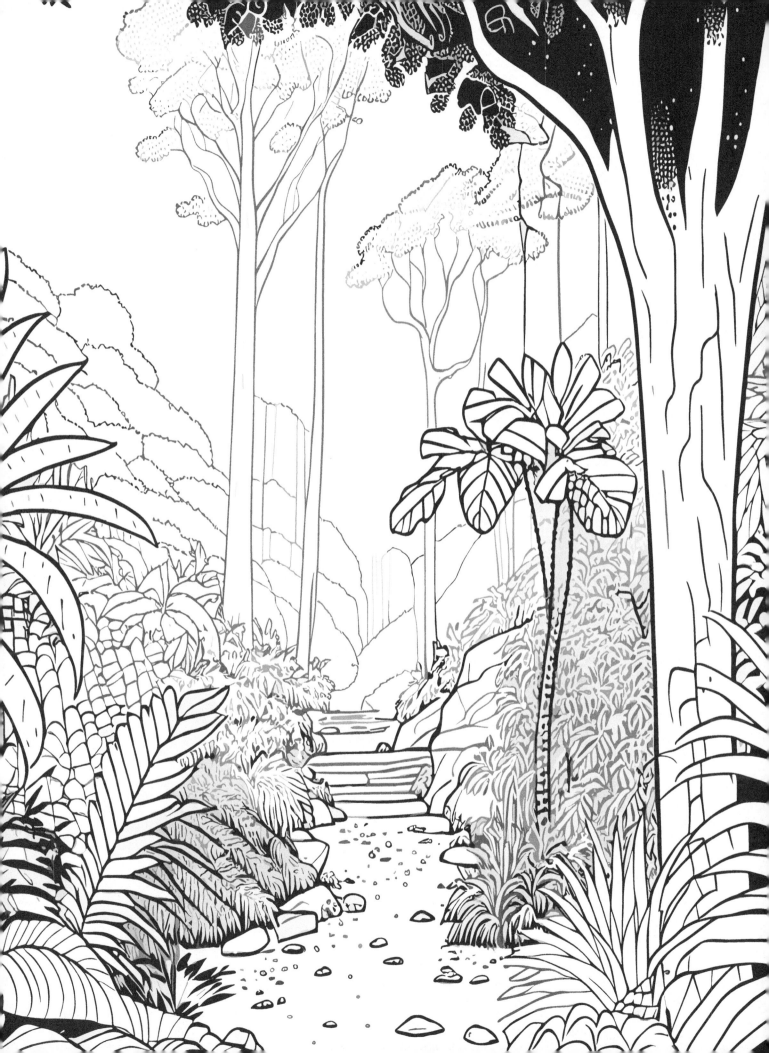

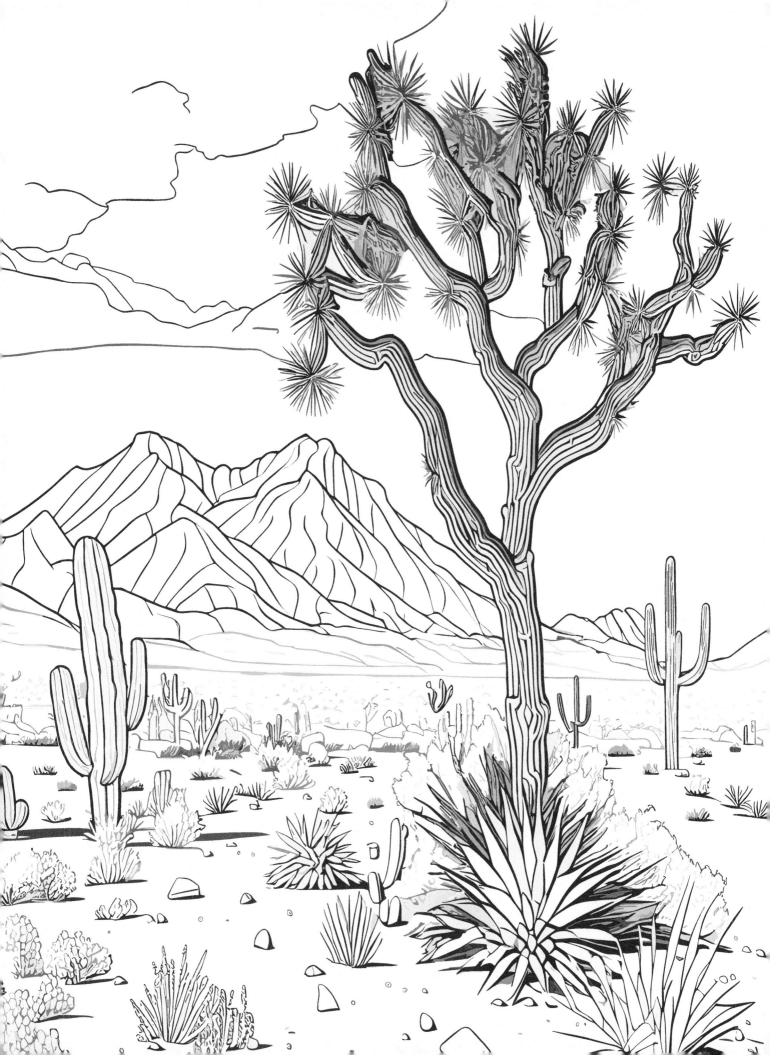

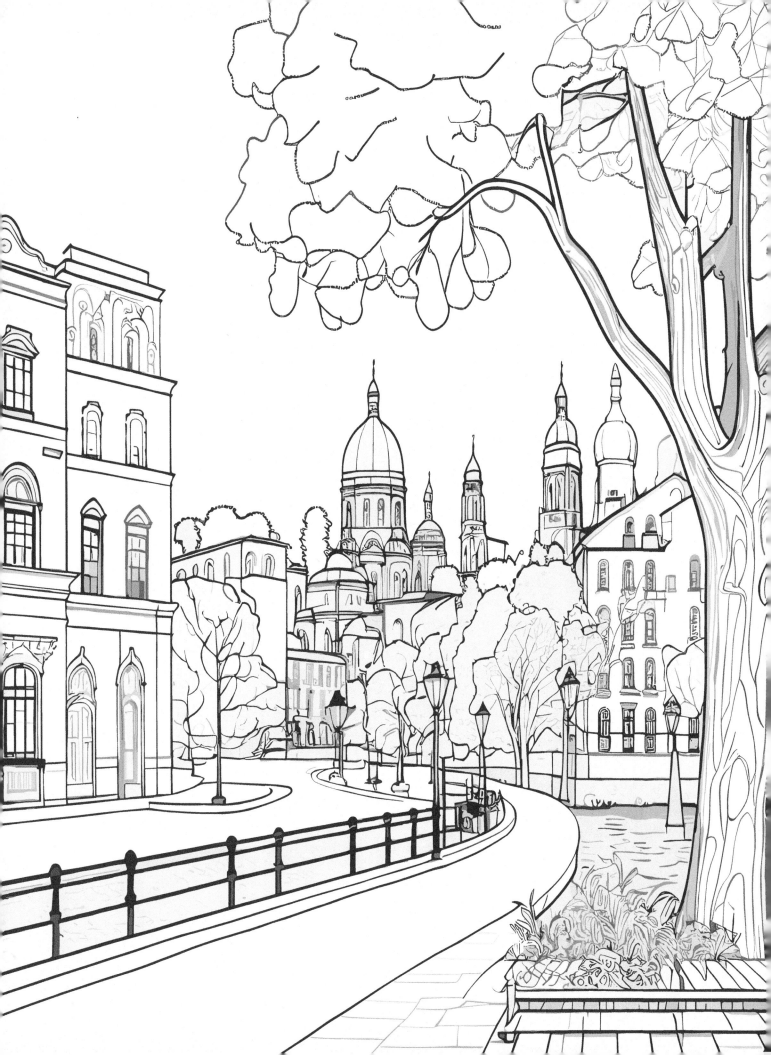

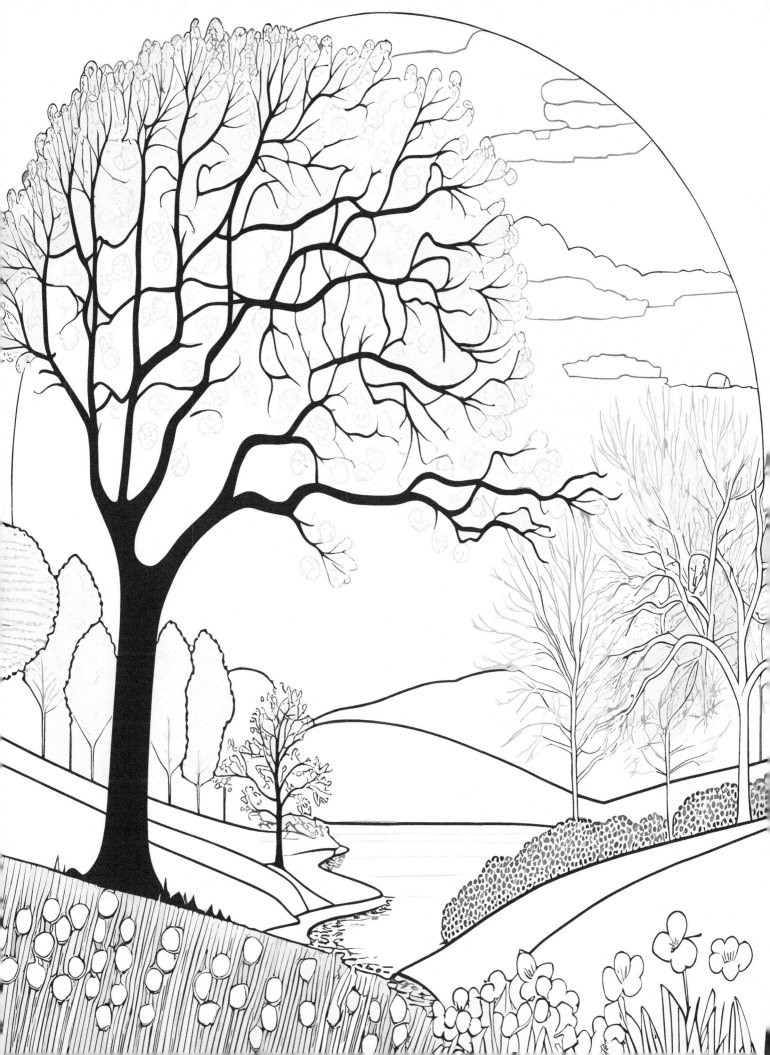

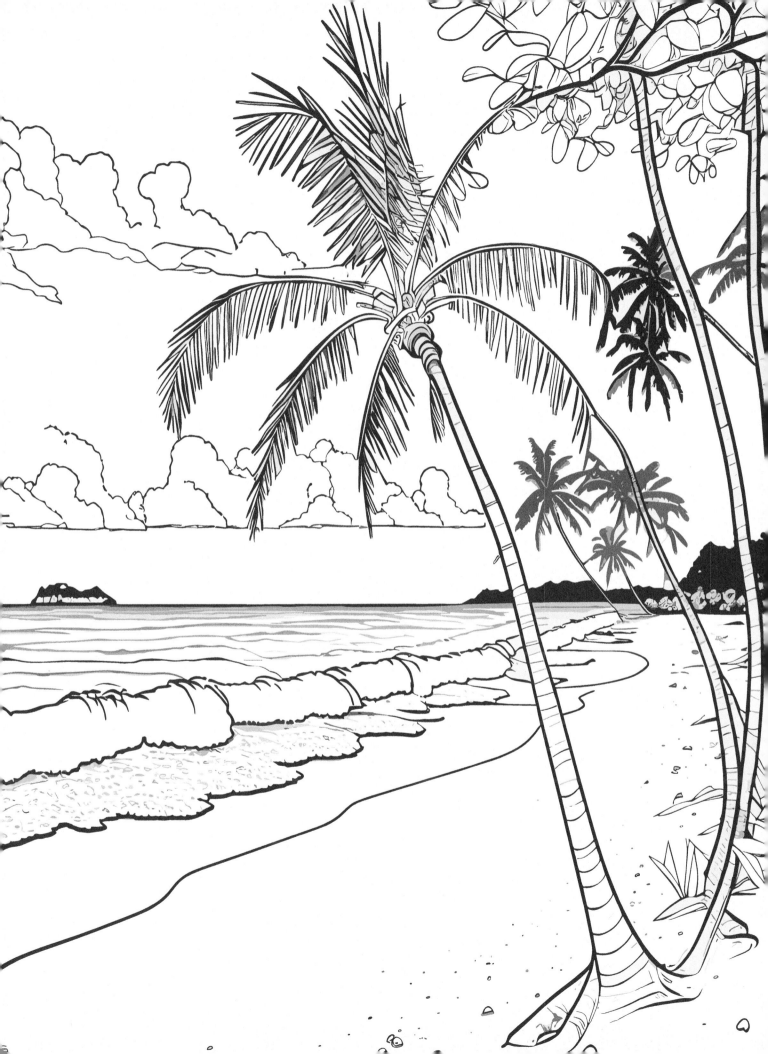

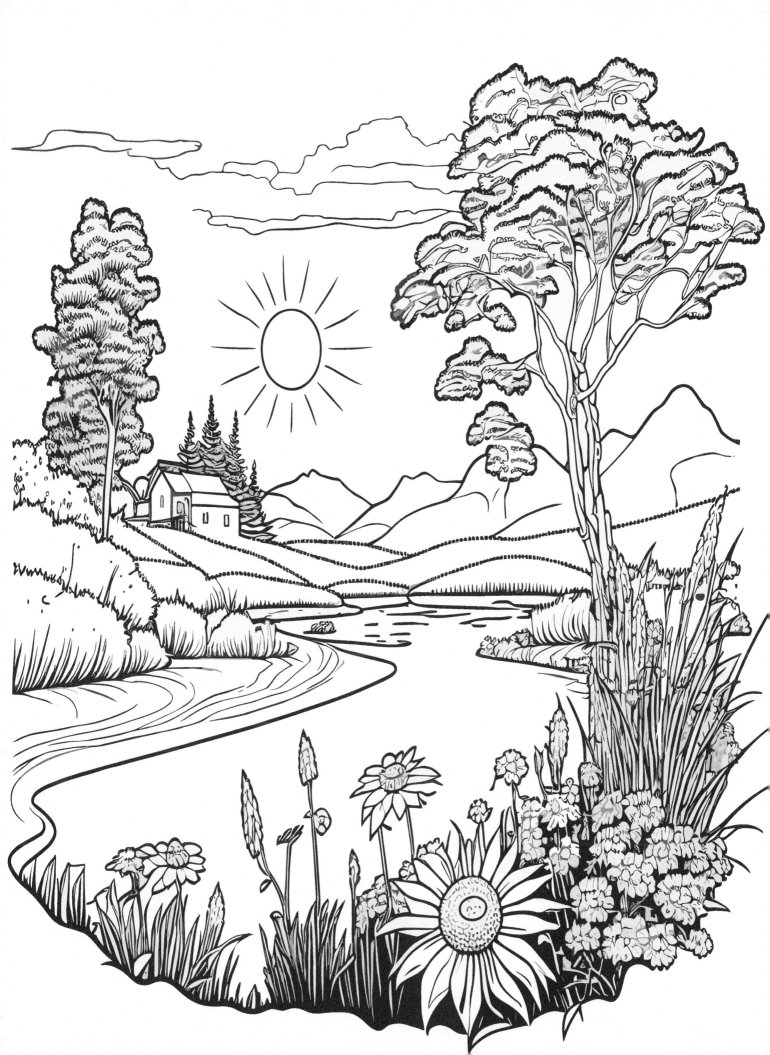

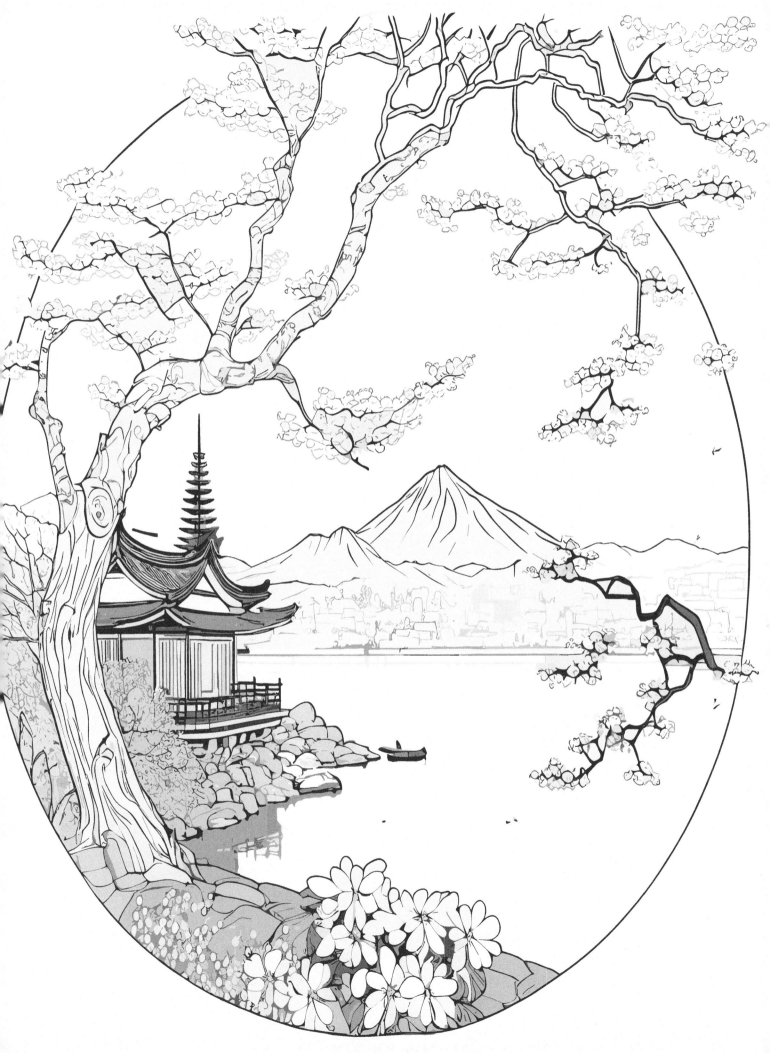

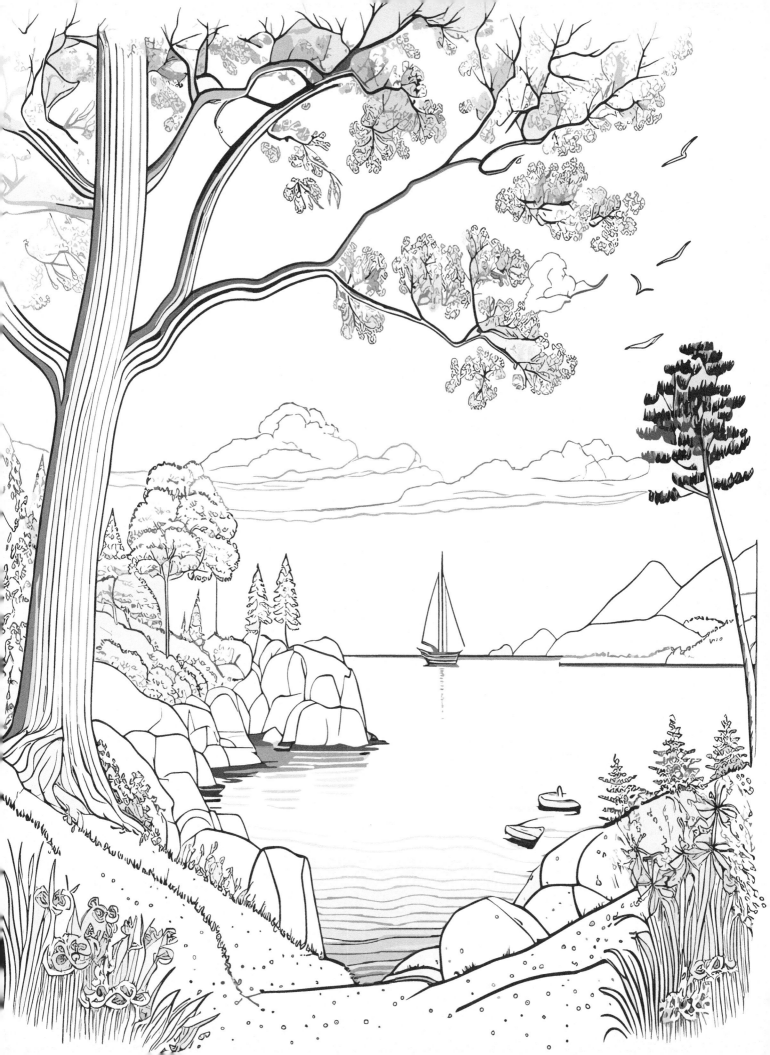

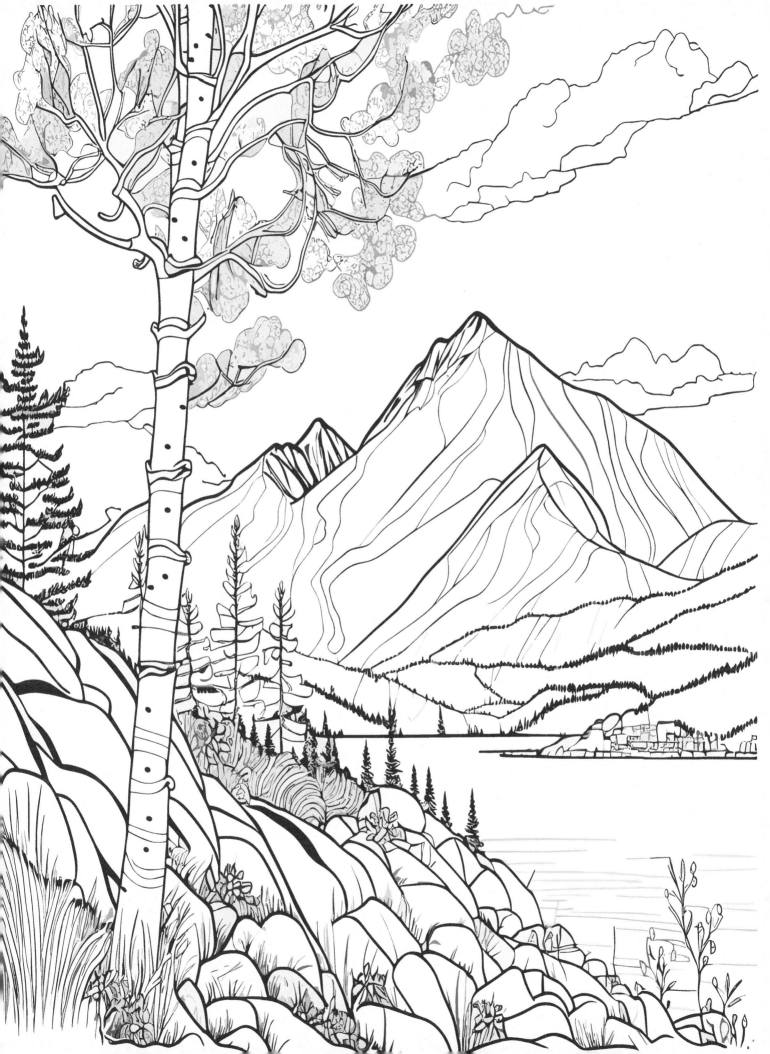

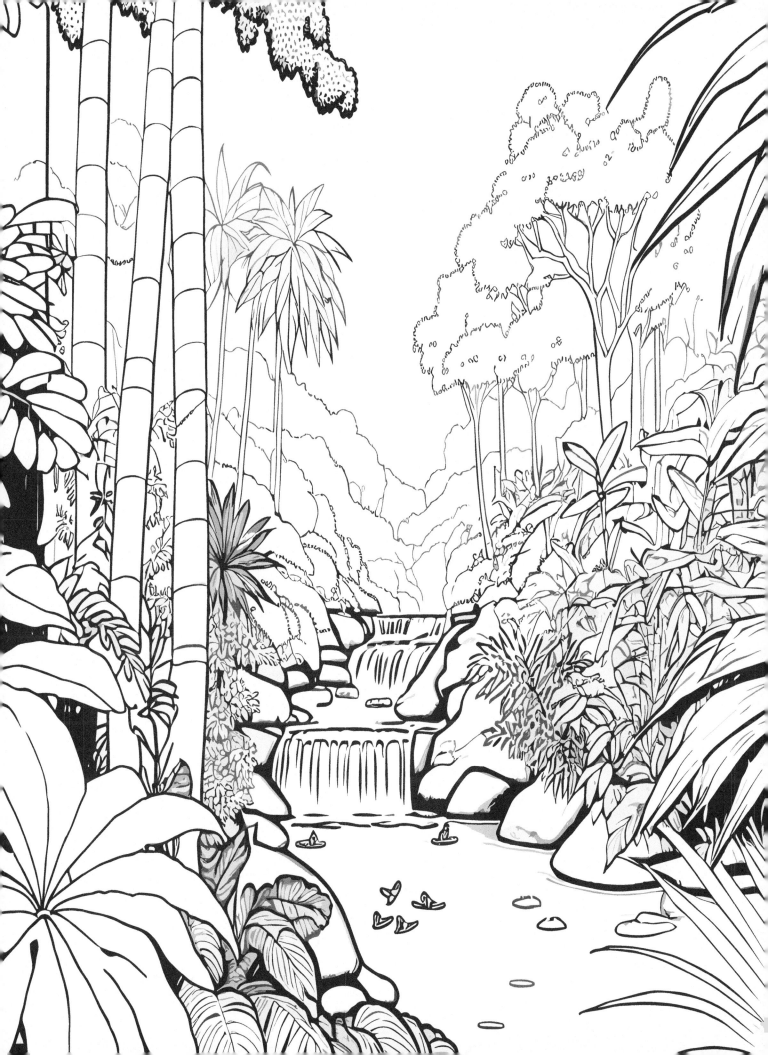

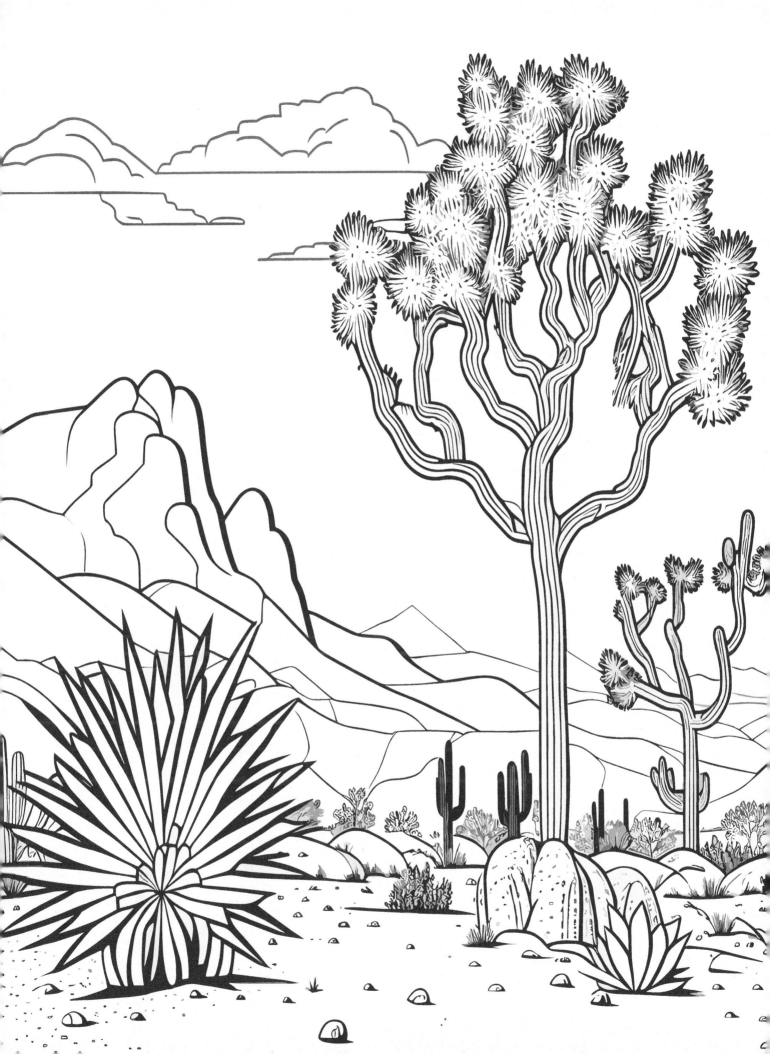

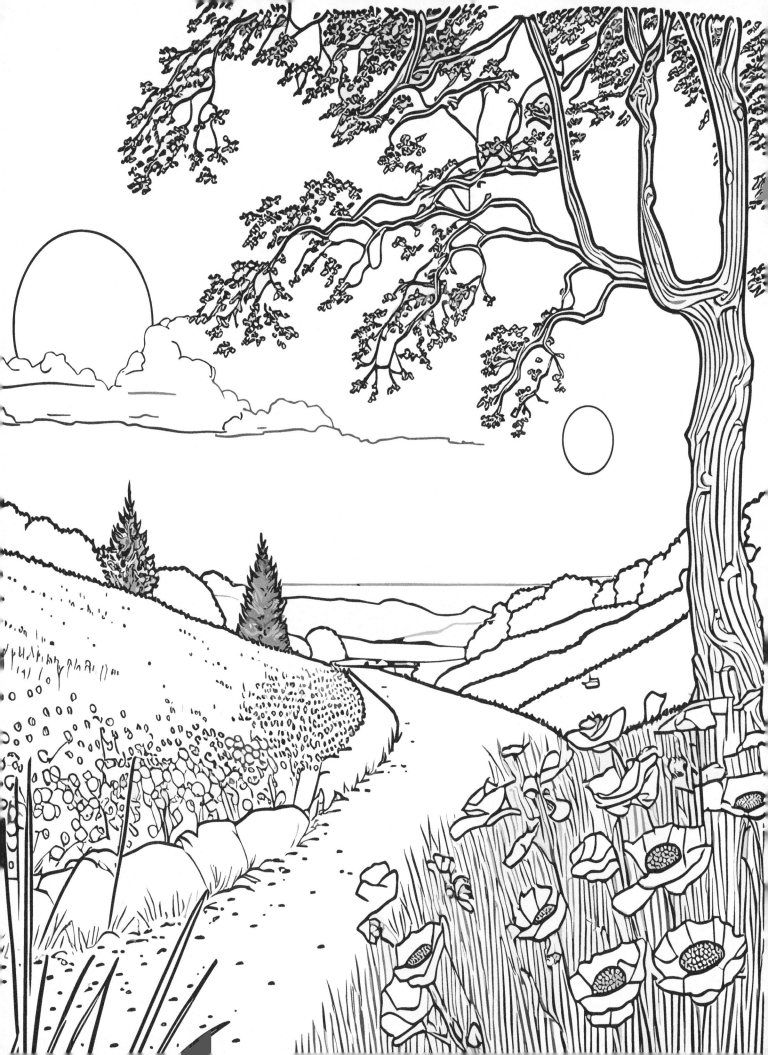

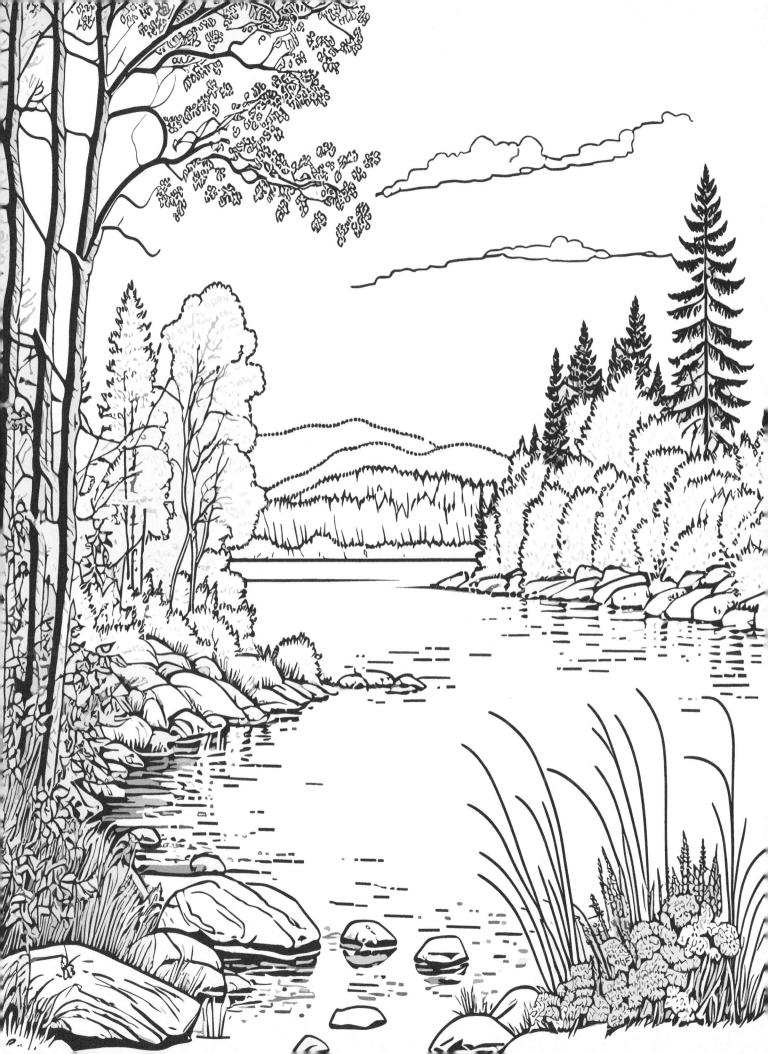

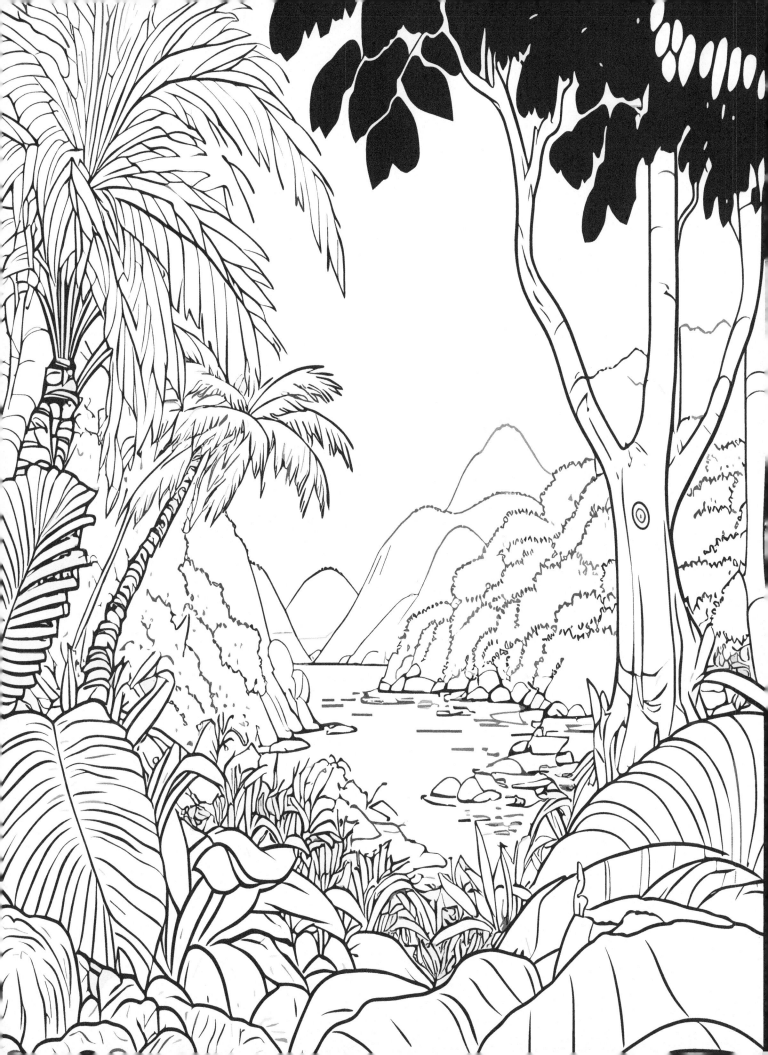

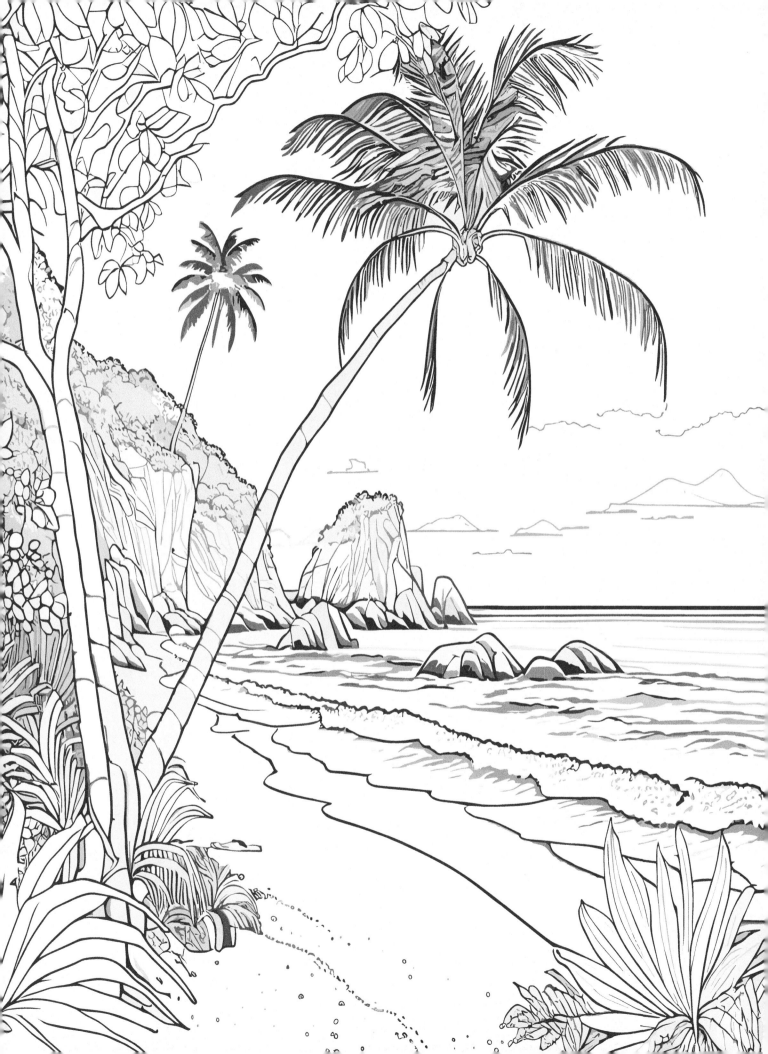

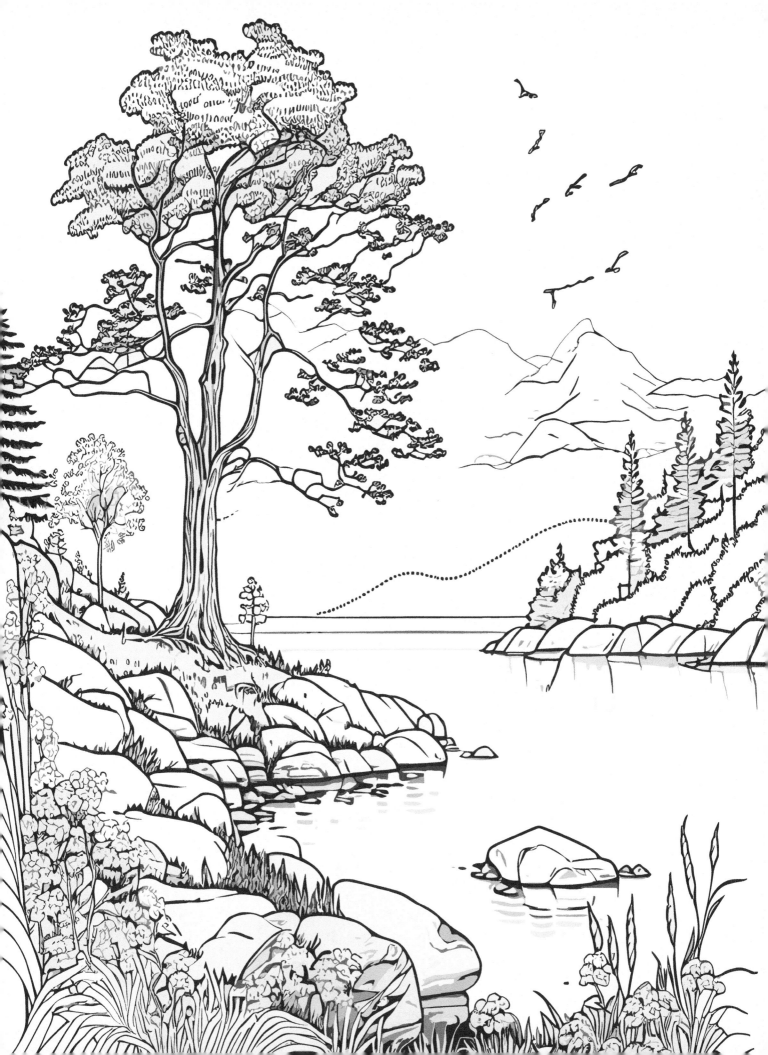

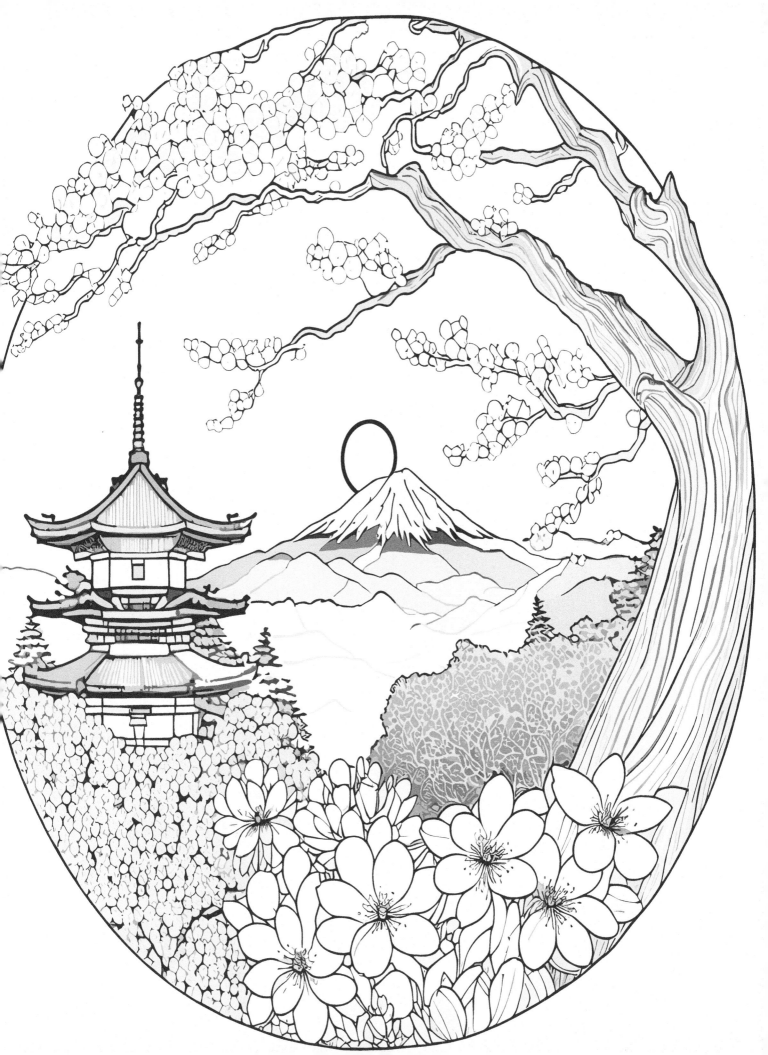

First of all, thank you for purchasing this book
I hope that it added at value and quality to your everyday life.
If so, it would be really nice if you could
take some time to post a review on Amazon.

Your Feedback will be highly appreciated!